It is a dark November evening in 2001 and Dan Radcliffe is very nervous. He is only twelve, but he is famous. The first Harry Potter film, *Harry Potter and the Philosopher's Stone*, is at the cinema for the first time. 10,000 people are waiting in the street, near the cinema in London. They all want to see the actors; they all want to see Dan.

In the dark cinema, the film starts. Dan watches – and there he is! That night, the people in the cinema see the new face of the famous boy with the glasses. After that, for many people, Daniel Radcliffe – Dan to his friends and family – *is* Harry Potter.

J. K. Rowling's books are very famous, and Daniel Radcliffe is the face of Harry Potter. But who is the young actor? And is there a life for him after the films?

Life Before Harry Potter

Today, people in many countries know the young film actor's name and face. But how did he start? Did he always want to be an actor? And what did he do before Harry Potter?

On 23 July 1989, Daniel Radcliffe comes into the world. His mother and father live in London. His father works with writers, and his mother works with actors. She knows about the lives of child actors; sometimes their lives can be very difficult. Dan's mother and father don't want a child actor in the house; they want a normal, happy child. Daniel *is* normal. He has a normal life at school. One year he is in a school play. He plays the part of an animal!

Because of their jobs, Dan's mother and father know a lot of people in film and television. One of them wants to make

Young Daniel in David Copperfield

a television film of Charles Dickens's famous book *Oliver Twist* and he has an important question for the Radcliffe family. Does Dan want to act in the film? His mother and father say no. But then a family friend comes to the Radcliffes. Does Dan want to be in a BBC television series of Dickens's book *David Copperfield*?

This time, Dan's mother and father say yes. Dan goes and talks to the director of the series. Then he has an audition for the part. He has five auditions, and then ... the answer is yes! On television, Dan is the new David Copperfield.

This is Dan's first job, and he is only ten at the time. He is nervous on the first day because many famous actors are in the series. One of them is Maggie Smith. Later, Dan is going to work with her again in the Harry Potter films; she plays the teacher Minerva McGonagall.

The first part of *David Copperfield* is on television in Britain on 25 December 2000 – Christmas Day. People love it, and they love the young actor with the big blue eyes.

After *David Copperfield*, Dan works on a Hollywood film, *The Tailor of Panama*. Again, he works with very famous actors. American Jamie Lee Curtis and Australian Geoffrey Rush are his mother and father in the film. Jamie has a book with her on the film set. It is a children's book about a young wizard ... Harry Potter. In her book, writer J. K. Rowling says, 'Harry has a thin face ... black hair and green eyes.'

Dan's eyes are blue, not green. But, for Jamie, young Dan is the right actor for the job in a Harry Potter film. She talks about this to Dan's mother.

Daniel in his Harry Potter glasses

The Young Wizard

In 1997, J. K. Rowling's first book, *Harry Potter and the Philosopher's Stone*, arrives in book shops. Readers love this story of a young wizard's first year at Hogwarts School. Now people in many countries know about Harry Potter.

One of these people is film maker David Heyman. David is British, but at this time he is working with people in Los Angeles. He wants to make a film of J. K. Rowling's book and he starts to talk to writers and directors.

Readers wait for book two in the series, and *Harry Potter and the Chamber of Secrets* arrives in 1998. Children love this book – and book three, *Harry Potter and the Prisoner of Azkaban*. Their mothers and fathers love the stories, too; 40% of J. K. Rowling's readers are not children. For the first time, many children like putting on their glasses because of Harry Potter!

In Los Angeles, David Heyman has a writer, Steve Kloves, and a director, Chris Columbus. There is a lot of money for the film of the first Harry Potter book . . . but no Harry Potter.

The film makers don't want a famous actor. They want a 'new face', and they want a British child. A lot of young actors have auditions for the part, but the film makers can't find the right child.

Then, one night, Heyman and Kloves go to a play in London. There is a family behind them – the Radcliffes, with their son, Daniel. Columbus and Kloves know Dan's father and they start to talk to him about the Harry Potter film.

The day after that, Dan visits the film set. Then he has an audition for the part of Harry Potter. Dan is very nervous,

Emma, Daniel and Rupert

but he goes for two auditions after this. Then they telephone him – Dan has the job. He is the new Harry Potter! He is very happy and doesn't sleep well that night.

Now a very important person watches a short film of Dan's acting – writer J. K. Rowling. She is happy with the young actor in the part. After that, Dan reads her books again. He wants to understand Harry very well.

They start to film in September 2000, in England. On the first day, there are a lot of actors and workers on the set and Dan is very nervous. But he isn't the only young actor there.

Rupert Grint is playing Harry Potter's friend, Ron Weasley. Rupert is eleven, too. Emma Watson – Harry's clever friend Hermione Granger in the story – is only ten. This is Rupert and Emma's first film. The three children are quickly good friends.

Film makers often work very long days. But child actors can't work all day because they have school work. For 130 days, the young actors work on the set of *Harry Potter and the Philosopher's Stone* and do their school work, too. In that time, Dan doesn't often see his old school friends on weekdays. But he likes his new friends, Rupert and Emma, and the three young actors have a good time.

Dan likes acting with the special effects. He likes the part of the film with the game of Quidditch. But life on a film set isn't always interesting for actors. For a lot of the time, they sit and wait. Sometimes Dan listens to music and sometimes he watches films at these times. He likes playing jokes on the set, too. Sometimes Rupert and Emma play jokes on him.

The three young actors with J.K. Rowling

The World Loves Harry Potter!

Some newspapers don't like the film, but many, many people love it. Dan's face is on television and in newspapers all the time. (He is always in glasses because Harry Potter has glasses. But Dan doesn't have glasses in his normal life!) He goes from country to country and talks about the film. This is a new world for him now. He is a famous actor in a big film. But Dan is the same boy. He likes music and television; he likes to see his old friends.

Dan doesn't have a lot of time for his friends because the film makers want to start work on *Harry Potter and the Chamber of Secrets*. In November 2001, Dan is on the film set again. He isn't nervous this time. Many of the actors from the first film are playing their parts again, and the film's director is the same – Chris Columbus.

After this film, Dan wants a new job. In November 2002, he is in a play in London. He is only in the play for one night. This is his first time on stage, but Dan likes it. He wants to go on stage again.

For months in 2003, Dan is filming *Harry Potter and the Prisoner of Azkaban*. There is a new director for film three – the Mexican director Alfonso Cuarón. Before work starts on the film, Cuarón gives Dan, Rupert and Emma a job; they write about Harry, Ron and Hermione for him.

Dan is very happy because the actor Gary Oldman is in this film. He plays Sirius Black, an old friend of Harry Potter's father. Dan loves Oldman's film work.

Harry Potter and the Prisoner of Azkaban arrives in cinemas in June 2004, but the film makers start to film *Harry Potter*

Rupert, Emma and Daniel at Harry Potter and
the Goblet of Fire

and the Goblet of Fire before this. Dan, Rupert and Emma aren't child actors now; they are teenagers. But some parts of the film are difficult for a young actor; Harry has to give a dead boy to the boy's father.

Harry Potter and the Goblet of Fire is in the cinemas in November, 2005. Film five in the series, *Harry Potter and the Order of the Phoenix,* arrives in 2007. In this film Harry Potter, a teenager, has his first kiss. This is Dan's first kiss in a film, too!

The Teenager Behind the Films

Today, Daniel Radcliffe is a famous young man with a lot of money. He makes films. He visits many countries. There are books about him. (You have got one in your hands!) Can he have the normal life of a teenager, too?

The answer is yes ... sometimes. Dan lives in London with his mother and father, and he sees many of his old friends. He likes watching films and TV – he loves the American television series *The Simpsons*. He likes watching football and listening to music. He likes playing with his two dogs, Blinka and Nugget. He never watches his films after their first night in cinemas, and he doesn't read newspaper stories about the Harry Potter films – or about Daniel Radcliffe.

Many people like him because he can be a 'normal' teenager. Many girls like him, too ... Dan gets a lot of letters from girls. Some girls want to go out with him because he is famous. Sometimes girls come to the door of his house in London. Dan's mother is friendly to them but she always sends them away.

Daniel on MTV

What Now for Dan?

There are only seven Harry Potter books. Daniel Radcliffe can't always play Harry Potter. In 2006, Dan starts to try new work. He makes a film in Australia, *December Boys*, about four boys on holiday near the sea. He is in *Extras*, a television series, and in a TV film, *My Boy Jack*. In *Extras* he plays 'Daniel Radcliffe'. There are a lot of jokes about him – the 'Daniel Radcliffe' in the show thinks about women all the time. Dan didn't have a problem with these jokes. In *My Boy Jack* he plays the son of the writer Rudyard Kipling.

In 2007, Dan goes back to the London stage again, but this time he takes a big part in a difficult play. Dan plays the teenager Alan Strang in Peter Schaffer's *Equus*. In the play Strang is an angry young man with a lot of problems. For part of the play, Daniel is naked on stage. Actor Richard Griffiths is in the play, too, and Daniel knows him from the Harry Potter films. Daniel is very good in the play.

What work is Dan going to do after Harry Potter? This young actor likes to try new parts.

Perhaps he isn't going to be an actor. 'I love English, reading and writing,' Dan says. Is he going to be a writer? He loves watching films; perhaps he is going to be a director. He likes playing music; perhaps he is going to do that.

But Dan is always going to remember Harry Potter. Dan likes Harry. Harry is a wizard, but he is a normal person, too.

Dan on stage in Equus

ACTIVITIES

Pages 1–7

Before you read

1 Look at the Word List at the back of the book. What are the words in your language?

2 Talk about these questions.

    a What do you know about Daniel Radcliffe?

    b What do you know about the Harry Potter books and films?

    c Why do many people love the Harry Potter stories?

While you read

3 Are these sentences right (✓) or wrong (✗)?

    a Daniel Radcliffe's mother and father work with writers.

    b Dan lives in London.

    c Dan's mother wanted him to act in *Oliver Twist*.

    d *Harry Potter and the Philosopher's Stone* was Dan's first film.

    e Dan didn't audition for Harry Potter.

    f Dan was nervous on the first day on the set of *Harry Potter and the Philosopher's Stone*.

After you read

4 Work with two friends.

    Student A: You are David Heyman. You want Dan to be Harry Potter. Talk to the Radcliffes.

    Student B: You are Dan's mother or father. You want a normal, happy son. Talk to David Heyman, and to Dan.

    Student C: You are Dan. You want to be in the film. Talk to your mother/father and to David Heyman.

Pages 8–15

Before you read

5 Talk to a friend.

    a Did you see *Harry Potter and the Philosopher's Stone*? Did you like it? Why (not)?

b Which Harry Potter films do you like? Which do you not like? Why?

c Can a young actor with a lot of money have a normal life, too? Why (not)?

While you read

6 Who is it? Write the numbers, 1–6.

a	the director of *Harry Potter and the Chamber of Secrets*	**1)**	Daniel Radcliffe
b	the director of *Harry Potter and the Prisoner of Azkaban*	**2)**	Chris Columbus
		3)	Alfonso Cuarón
c	Hermione Granger	**4)**	Gary Oldman
d	Ron Weasley	**5)**	Rupert Grint
e	Sirius Black	**6)**	Emma Watson
f	Alan Strang in *Equus*		

After you read

7 Which words are right?

a Daniel likes *The Simpsons / swimming*.

b Daniel has two *cars / dogs*.

c In *Harry Potter and the Order of the Phoenix* Harry has his first *dance / kiss*.

d Harry Potter is a *wizard / actor*.

Writing

8 Is Daniel Radcliffe the right actor for Harry Potter? Why (not)? Write about it.

9 Think of some questions for Daniel. Write a letter to him and ask your questions.

10 Write about one of the photos in this book. What can you see?

11 You want to be an actor. Do want to work in film, television or plays? Why? Write about it.

Answers for the activities in this book are available from the Penguin Readers website. A free Activity Worksheet is also available from the website. Activity Worksheets are part of the Penguin Teacher Support Programme, which also includes Progress Tests and Graded Reader Guidelines. For more information, please visit: www.penguinreaders.com.